AF552375

COVER PHOTO

Seaman, "The Dog Who Helped Explore America," is depicted with other heroes of the Lewis and Clark Expedition, in this statue in Great Falls, Montana, by famed artist Robert Scriver. With Seaman are York (kneeling), Captain William Clark and Captain Meriwether Lewis. (Photo courtesy Dale Burk)

THE DOG
Who Helped Explore America

By R.W. "Rib" Gustafson

THE DOG WHO HELPED EXPLORE AMERICA

R. W. "Rib" Gustafson

Library of Congress Catalog Card Number: 98-61368

ISBN 0-012299-75-4

Published by R. W. Gustafson, Route 1, Box 136,
Conrad, Montana 59425
in cooperation with *Montana Legacy Series*,
an imprint of Stoneydale Press Publishing Company, Stevensville, Montana

Designed, typesetting and other prepress work by Stoneydale Press.

Cover photo by Dale A. Burk

Illustrations by Mike DayRider and Dr. Jim Scott.

Distributed by Stoneydale Press Publishing Company,
523 Main Street, Stevensville, Montana 59870
Phone: 1-800-735-7006

First Edition

Manufactured in the United States of America

TABLE OF CONTENTS

ACKNOWLEDGEMENTS

I WOULD LIKE to make special acknowledgement of several individuals in regard to *The Dog Who Helped Explore America*. They include:

- Dr. Jim Scott
- Mike DayRider
- My family
- Dean Hellinger
- Bob Scriver
- Dale Burk

DEDICATION

I dedicate this book to our nine grandchildren:

Connor
Nina *Mark*
Luke
Evan
Ben
Erika
Sinda
Greta

and hopefully, more to come........

FOREWORD

LET ME INTRODUCE my father's book. My father has a keen interest in Lewis and Clark. When I was eight years old he began reading The Journals of Lewis and Clark edited by Bernard DeVoto. Whenever he found what he thought was an extremely humorous or interesting passage he would dog-ear the page and assign me that particular section to read the next day. "Here, read this, just imagine." I never realized there was a dog on the expedition until he authored this children's book, but with all the dog-ears in the broken-spined book I should have. His knowledge of the Expedition's travels in our immediate area of the Golden Triangle was extensive and he was proud to say he'd

Seaman with York. Detail from the statue by Robert Scriver in Great Falls, Montana.

gleaned it all from the original Journals.

I frequently traveled with him all over the upper headwaters of the Missouri. I assisted him with his ambulatory veterinary practice, chasing through the big country from one animal to another all through the big open, ranch to ranch, farm to farm. Big sky is one thing, big country is another. From the foothills of the eastern Rocky Mountain front you could see the country forever, the same big country Lewis and Clark witnessed before the onslaught of progress. The land of course has changed significantly since the Corps of Discovery passed through. Through my dad's vivid imagination, what remained of the country, and the journal writings, my dad nurtured a feeling of how it really might have been before Manifest Destiny forever altered the environment. His insight allowed me a child's naive outlook of how things were before cattle, wheat, and fences replaced the buffalo and wolves and Indians. The exploration by Lewis and Clark became the beginning of the end of Indians mingling with the land. The Journals became somewhat of a bible, our reference into the past we missed. Every time we crossed the Expedition's path he would point out geographic landmarks and what had happened then, and there, and why. How the country once was in its undisturbed evolved splendor. I don't remember him ever mentioning the Newfoundland. But now I know. Newfoundland it was, indeed. If this book sparks other children's interest in the pristine past as much as my dad sparked mine I assure you it will be an invaluable experience for you and your child, especially if you have your own dog.

Dog was the first species man domesticated. The Indians of the region had dogs and by the time Meriwether and his Newfoundland passed through they had horses also. How fitting of the Corps to bring a dog. If not for companionship, protection, portage, and leadership, then perhaps most importantly they brought a dog to relate to the Indians. This significantly helped allow them safe passage through the wilds of that time. Nothing better than a big, black, happy dog to impress the natives. This was a relationship between man and animal the Indians knew. On seeing how the white army, like them, related to dog allowed a peaceful connection. So it was the dog that initially impressed the Indians and thus helped the explorers get their food and supplies safely through prairies and mountains, then the Indians' domain. The importance of the dog to the journey through what we now know as America has never been so delightfully acknowledged until this book. Imagine the native people's surprise and acceptance to see that, like themselves, these foreigners must have had merit in realizing the importance of a dog to man. Without this connection, this domesticated wolf factor, I realize that

Lewis and Clark may have never made it to the Pacific and back.

Sit back, get your dog on your children's lap, and have a good read. You and yours will better understand the importance of man's best friend to all peoples alike through all of man's time on earth. The dog has not only survived, but has flourished through to the present. Perhaps better than any species of all, dog has helped all peoples understand each others inner emotions of existence. How fitting it is that the dog has now been brought to the attention it deserves for ensuring the success of the journey. Without Seaman, the Corps of Discovery may have not discovered anything at all. Slowly but surely the country moved from wolf to dog. It makes one wonder where would we all be today without our dogs to show us the meaning and purpose of nature and life itself?

Enjoy.

Sid Gustafson, DVM

INTRODUCTION

AS A VETERINARIAN, I am interested in all animals. This historical episode of Captain Lewis's dog, "Seaman", intrigued me when I first read about him. Newfoundland retrievers are believed to be the only dog indigenous to North America.

The references to the escapades of this canine are taken from the original Journals of Captains Lewis and Clark, Bernard DeVoto's excerpts from the Journals, Sergeant Gass' diary and other historians.

The last reference to Seaman was his excitement at being charged by a moose as Captain Lewis crossed the Continental Divide on his return journey to St. Louis. Since his diary is almost non-existent after this point, I took the privilege of having him be with Captain Lewis as he and three of his most capable soldiers had the skirmish with the Blackfeet in which two Blackfeet were killed.

It wasn't long after this when Captain Lewis was shot in the butt by one of his own men and spent most of the return journey lying on his stomach as Seaman watched over him. I jokingly refer to this as Montana's first recorded hunting accident. Since Cruzette, his most trusted boatman, was partially blind, the accident is understandable. This same man was an accomplished musician and furnished enjoyable music to the Corps on their journey and also to the large number of Indian friends in the progress of the Corps of Discovery. The dancing and jigging of the soldiers, even after hours of exhaustive labors, added to the spirit which the Corps exhibited. I nearly named this book "The Dog and the Fiddle."

I have taken the privilege of

adding my own happy ending to the story in which Pomp and Seaman spent many happy days together after Captain Lewis's unfortunate demise.

Some of the events may vary as to the exact time and place, but this simple book was written to encourage young and old to delve into the history of our great nation.

R. W. "Rib" Gustafson
Conrad, Montana

MY NAME IS Seaman; I am a Newfoundland Retriever purchased by my master, Captain Meriwether Lewis, in 1803 in Pittsburgh, Pennsylvania, while he was waiting for his boat to be built that would carry his men and supplies up the Missouri River. He gave $20.00 for me, which was a lot of money in those days and from that time on I was his constant companion on his travels to the Pacific Ocean and his return to St. Louis, Missouri, where the trip began and ended.

Ursus Horribilis — the great grizzly bear!

CAPTAIN LEWIS WAS the private secretary to President Thomas Jefferson, our third president. The United States of America had purchased a vast tract of land from France and he sent Captain Lewis on this mission to find out about the land, the people who lived there, and an easy route to the Pacific Ocean. Captain Lewis chose an old friend of his, Captain William Clark, as his co-captain for the trip which would then became known as the Lewis & Clark Expedition, or the Corps of

Discovery, which was the official name given them by President Jefferson.

THEY WERE THE first known white men to penetrate this vast land known as the Louisiana Purchase. These lands were inhabited by many tribes of Native Americans known as Indians and my adventures on this trip that took two years to complete were many and varied. I will relate some of them to you to help your knowledge of history.

FIRST OF ALL, as our boat floated down the Ohio River to the Mississippi River (the Ohio River is a tributary to the Mississippi, as is the Missouri River), I saw sights that will never be seen again. Squirrels were migrating across the river and I retrieved several of them for Captain Lewis and we had squirrel pie that night for supper.

DAY RIDER
'98

ALSO, THE SKIES were blackened by the migration of passenger pigeons, which are now extinct and will never be seen again. This is why we have to take care of the birds and animals that now live on our planet earth so that they can be heard and seen by future generations to come.

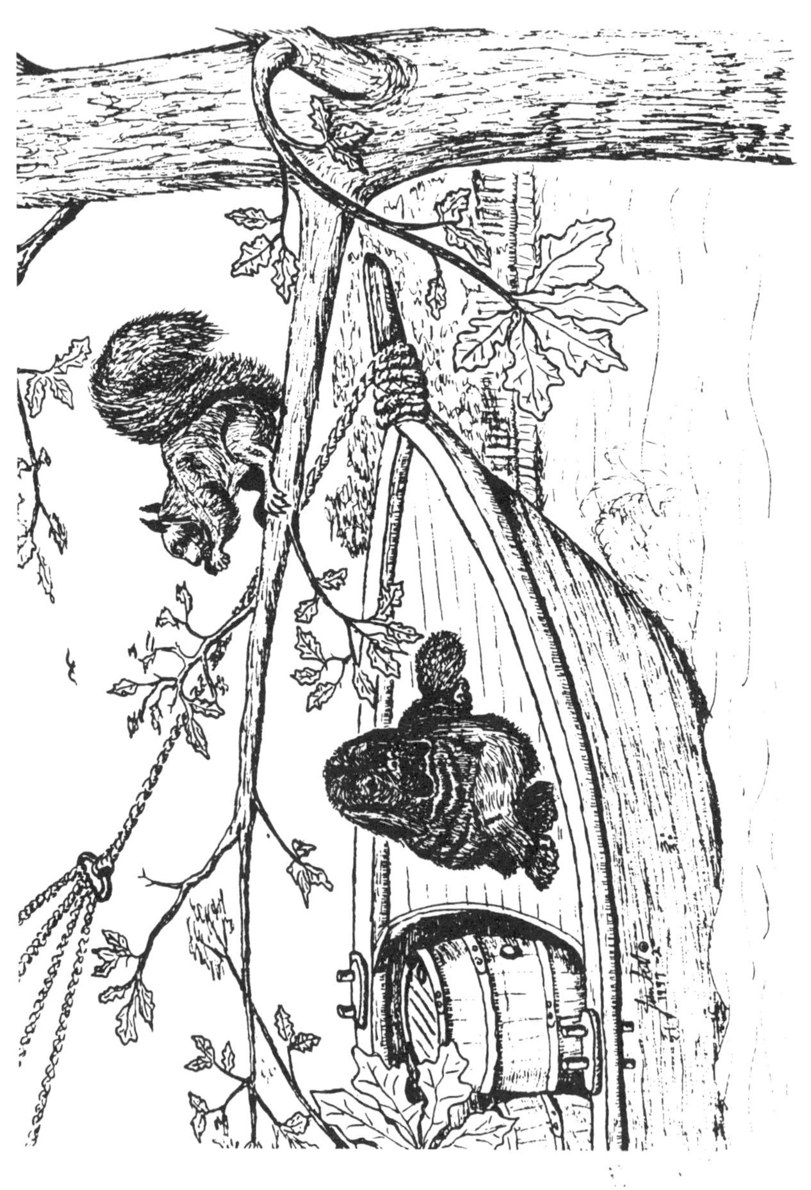

WE FLOATED DOWN down the river to the Mississippi and then up to St. Louis where we made preparation for our trip up the Missouri River in the spring of 1804. It was there that I became acquainted with a special friend, York, a black man who was Captain Clark's slave and would accompany us on the trip. York was a huge man and about to become one of the star attractions on the trip because of his color. The Indians would touch him and rub him to see if they could

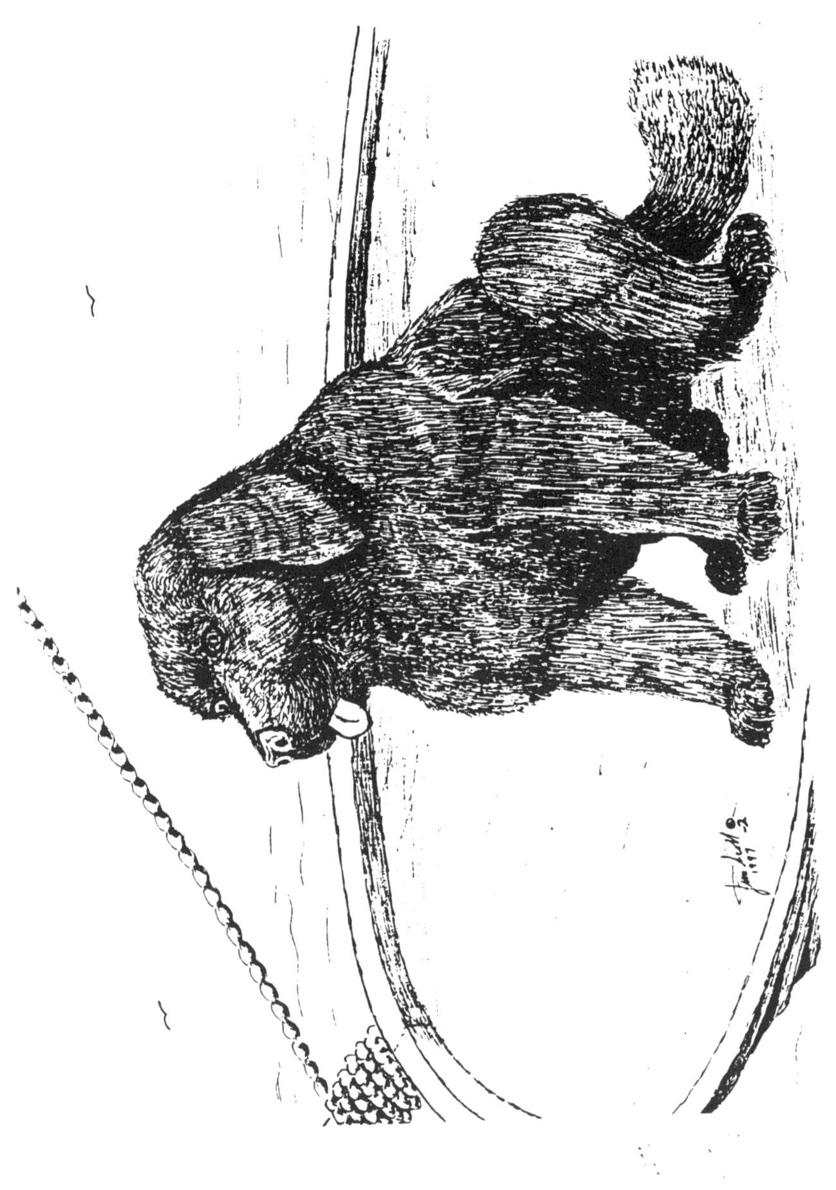

rub the black from his skin. I was also a star attraction because as dogs go, I was a giant among dogs. My black hair and huge size, about 150 pounds, made me the largest dog they had ever seen.

DAY RIDER
'98

LITTLE DID I know about the adventure that lay ahead for me; the new animals to be seen, the hardships endured, and the dangers involved in such a trip. I would stand on the prow of the boat or, if Captain Lewis chose, I would accompany him as he walked along the shore examining the flora and fauna of the land. Our first grave crisis came when the Sioux Indians tried to stop us from going up the river. Our soldiers were ready for a battle when the Indians finally backed down and we proceeded on.

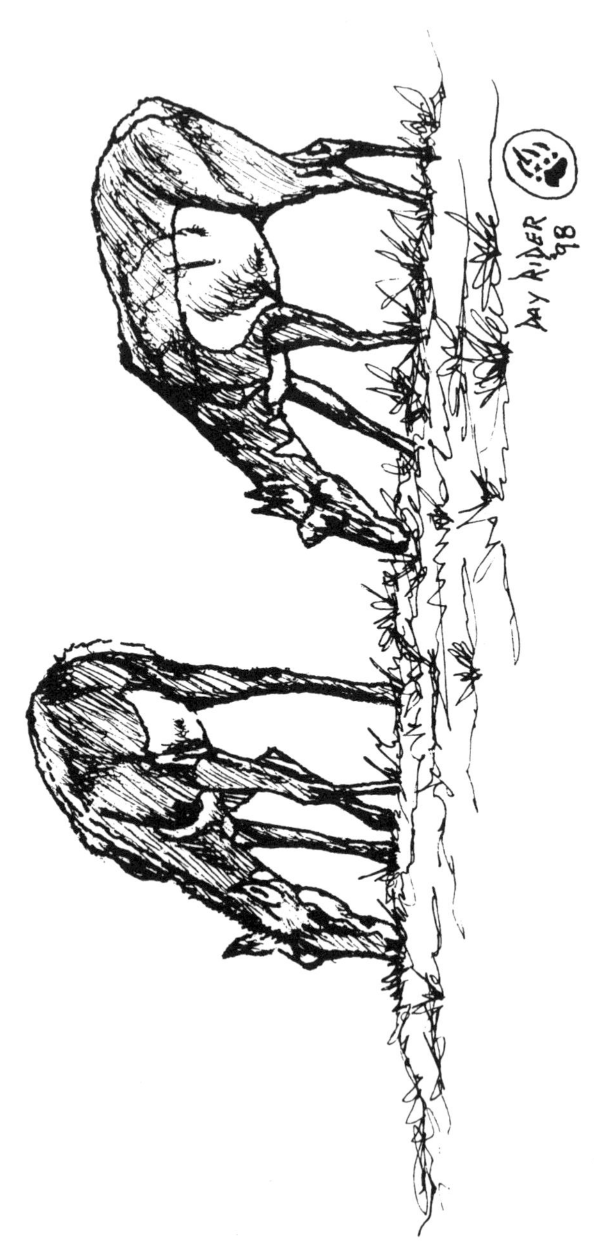

OUR NEXT BIG stop was with the Mandan Indians. Here we spent the winter of 1804-1805 and built a small fort and housing for our troops. It was here that I met my friend, Sacajawea, and her newborn baby who was given the nickname of "Pomp".

This is the carving of Captain William Clark's signature on Pompey's Pillar along the Yellowstone River.

POMPEY'S PILLAR

NEAR near Billings, Montana, where Captain Clark carved his name in 1806, is named after this baby who I looked after for the rest of our trip. When the ice melted in the spring, we proceeded on.

A huge grizzly bear ran one of our men into the river.

THE NEXT BIG stop was at the Great Falls of the Missouri River where we spent about three weeks building wagons pulled around the falls by the soldiers under the hot summer sun. We even put sails on the wagons to help us.

Seaman chased several bears away from our camp.

MY JOB AS the top dog of the exploration was to keep the many bears out of camp. Captain Lewis spent many an evening pulling the cactus thorns out of my feet. It was here also that I was bitten by a sharp-toothed beaver and nearly bled to death. My master, Captain Lewis, acted as my veterinarian and saved my life by putting a huge bandage on my leg and stopped the bleeding. After the portage around the Great Falls, we proceeded on.

WHEN THE LAND BELONGED TO GOD, *original oil by Charles M. Russell. Courtesy Montana Historical Society.*

WE CAME TO the Gates of the Mountains where I retrieved a deer swimming across the river for an additional venison feast for the soldiers. Next, we came to the Three Forks of the Missouri where Sacajewea had been captured as a young twelve-year-old girl by the Big Belly Indians. She was later sold to Charbonneau, along with her sister, before joining our exploration corps.

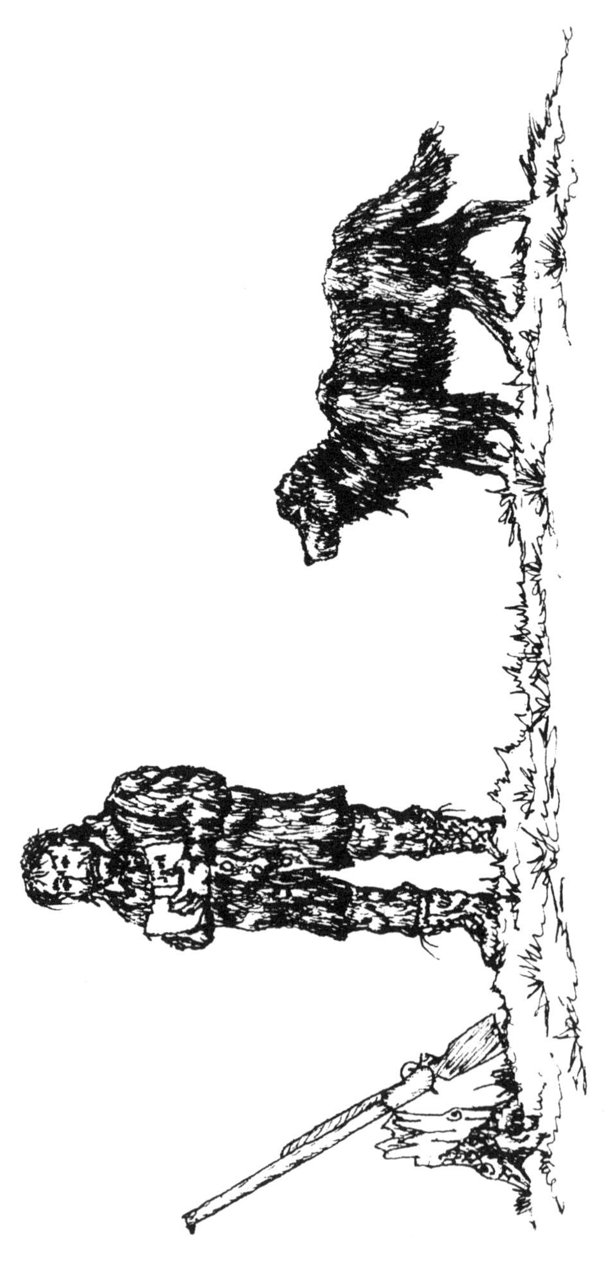

Rain or shine, Seaman was a constant companion of Captain Lewis.

WE PROCEEDED ON up the Jefferson River and soon came to a famous landmark named Beaverhead Rock, which Sacajewea recognized. Here we began to look for Sacajewea's relatives who had horses that we would purchase for our trip over the great Rocky Mountains. I accompanied my master, Captain Lewis, as we searched for natives and finally found them. Their chief was Sacajewea's brother, which was a great surprise to all.

LEWIS AND CLARK MEETING THE INDIANS AT ROSS' HOLE, *original oil by Charles M. Russell, 1912. Courtesy Montana Historical Society.*

HERE HORSES WERE purchased and we proceeded on by packing the horses for our great trip across the Rocky Mountains. When we crossed the mountains, we met many friendly Indian tribes. We finally came to the big rivers that flow to the Pacific Ocean. We turned over our horses to the Indians for safekeeping and proceeded on in boats and canoes which we made from the trunks of huge trees.

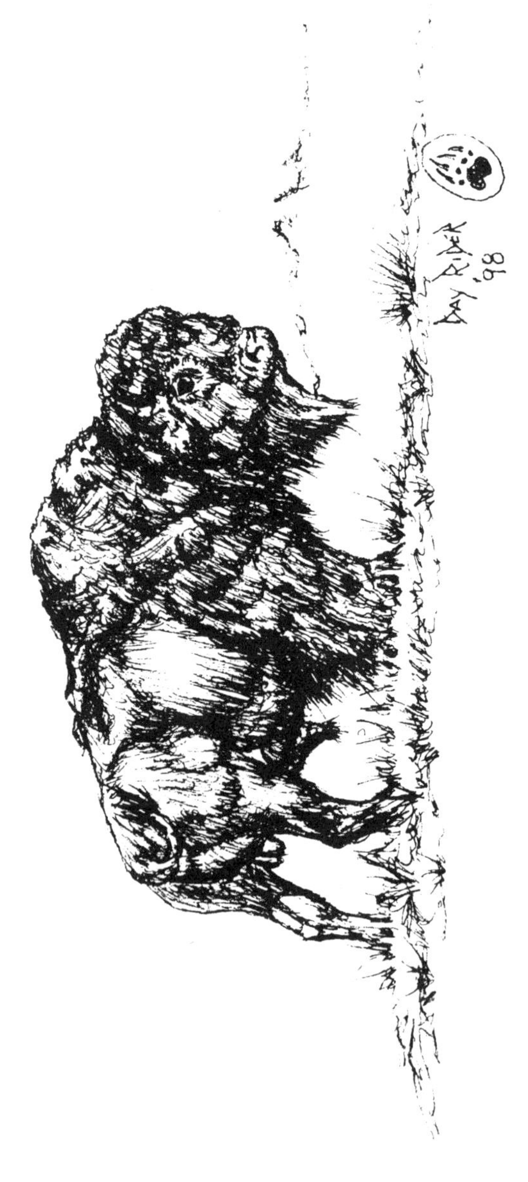
DAY RIDER '98

OUR FOOD CHANGED from buffalo to mainly fish that swim up the river to spawn. We met many Indian tribes that lived along the great river to the Pacific Ocean. We finally arrived at the Pacific Ocean and built a fort called Clatsop, named after the Indians who lived there. This was my home with my master, Captain Lewis, in the winter of 1805-1806. It rained nearly every day we were there.

IN MARCH, WE left Fort Clatsop and proceeded up the Columbia River on our trip home. I was a happy dog to be out of the rain and following my master as he walked along the shore.

DAY RIDER '98

ALL WENT WELL until April when the Indians stole me from my master. But Captain Lewis liked me so much he stopped the troops and sent soldiers after the Indians who had led me away from our camp. Three days later they rescued me from the Indians and I was happy to return to my master. After a difficult trip back over the mountains, which were still covered with snow, we arrived at Lolo Hot Springs where everyone bathed and rested.

EXALTED RULER, *original oil by Charles M. Russell, 1912. Courtesy C. M. Russell Museum, Great Falls, Montana.*

IN THE BITTERROOT Valley at a place called Traveller's Rest near the present town of Lolo, the captains made plans for the final trip home. Captain Clark left the main corps at the Three Forks of the Missouri and went over the Bozeman Pass to the Yellowstone River. The main group had retrieved their canoes on the headwaters of the Jefferson River and floated down to the Great Falls.

DAY RIDER
98

CAPTAIN LEWIS TOOK me and several men and went over the mountains to the Sun River. There I ran into a moose and became very excited. Captain Lewis calmed me and we proceeded on. When we arrived at the Great Falls of the Missouri, my master took me and three men and we proceeded north to the Marias River as a last resort to find a better passage. Here we camped at our last camp "Disappointment" before returning to the Great Falls.

THE MARIAS RIVER, *at the top left, flows into the broad expanse of the Missouri River. This is where Captain Lewis and his men rejoined with the rest of their party. (Photo courtesy Dale Burk)*

JUST AS WE started for our last leg of the journey, we encountered eight Blackfeet Indians. We camped with them overnight and at the break of day the next morning, the Indians attempted to steal our guns and horses. They were no match for the seasoned soldiers of the Expedition. Two Indians were killed and we took several of their horses to return to the Great Falls.

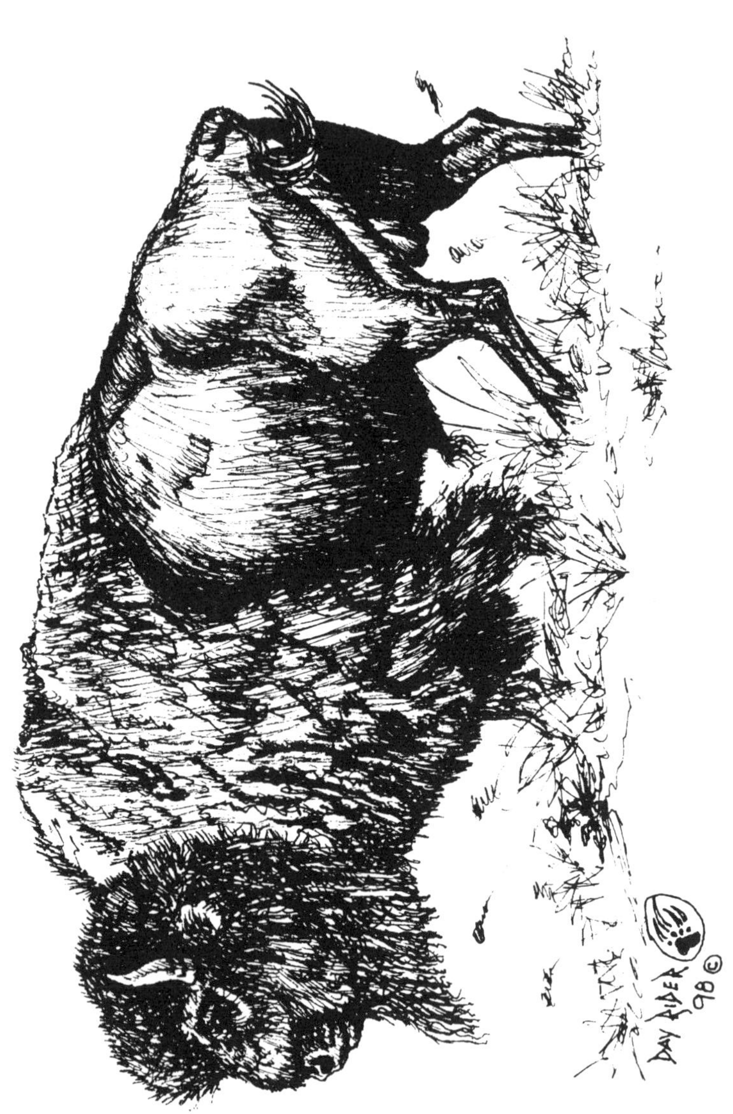
DAY RIDER 98©

THE PRAIRIES WERE filled with roaming buffaloes and early the next morning, we met with the soldiers floating down the river. We joined the Corps of Discovery and my exploring days were nearly over.

DAY RIDER '98

ONE MORE EVENT happened. Captain Lewis, my master, was shot in the buttocks by one of our own men. He had to lie on his stomach while his wounds healed on most of the entire trip home. I stood guard over him until he healed enough for a few daily walks.

WE ARRIVED HOME in September and I lived with my master until he died on a trip to Washington D.C. in 1809. I then moved in with Captain Clark and little Pomp to spend the rest of my days.

OTHER BOOKS BY R. W. GUSTAFSON, D.V.M.—

• *Under the Chinook Arch: Tales of a Montana Veterinarian*

• *Room to Roam: More Tales of a Montana Veterinarian*

Available at many bookstores, gift shops, or direct from the author by writing Route 1, Box 136, Conrad, Montana 59425.

Or, by contacting: STONEYDALE PRESS, 523 Main Street, Stevensville, Montana 59870 • Phone: 406-777-2729